INSPIRATIONAL ADULT
COLORING BOOK

LIVE
your
life
ON
PURPOSE

PRACTICAL WISDOM AND
ENCOURAGEMENT FROM
CRYSTAL PAINE,
THE MONEY-SAVING MOM®

MAJESTIC EXPRESSIONS
Relax, Refresh, Renew

BroadStreet
PUBLISHING

INTRODUCTION

Ever since I was a child, I adored coloring. I'm not really artistically gifted (if you ask me to sketch a specific animal, you probably wouldn't be able to tell what kind of animal it was when I was finished), so I'm drawn to coloring because I can turn out beautifully finished products—and all I have to do is color in the lines!

The quote and sayings in these pages are some of my very favorites. Many of them have motivated and challenged me for years. I'm excited to share two of my great loves with you on these pages—adult coloring and inspirational quotes.

Coloring is cathartic and calming for me. It's a break from the usual hustle and bustle of life. It's an opportunity to quietly create art (even if you don't possess talent!). It's an invitation to slow down and savor life a little more. It's also a fun activity you can share with your kids.

My hope in producing this coloring book is to encourage you to step back from the busyness of life and take a little time to do something to refuel and refresh your spirit and soul. Maybe you will re-awaken some long-lost creativity or child-like joy in your heart.

Turn on some music you love, make a mug of your favorite drink, grab some coloring pencils, or even crayons, and let's color!

Here's to many hours of making art—no skills required!

John Wooden.

Don't let what
you can't do
stop you from doing
what you can do.

If I'm too busy
to count my blessings,
I'm just plain too busy.

What you do today is important because you are exchanging a day of your life for it.

You are never too old
to set another goal
or to dream a new dream.

C. S. Lewis

Find the good
and praise it.

Either you run the day
or the day runs you.   — Jim Rohn

You can give
without loving,

but you cannot love
without giving.

D. Amy Carmichael

We can't help everyone, but everyone can help someone.

Ronald Reagan

Never get
so busy
making
a living
that you
forget to make
a life.

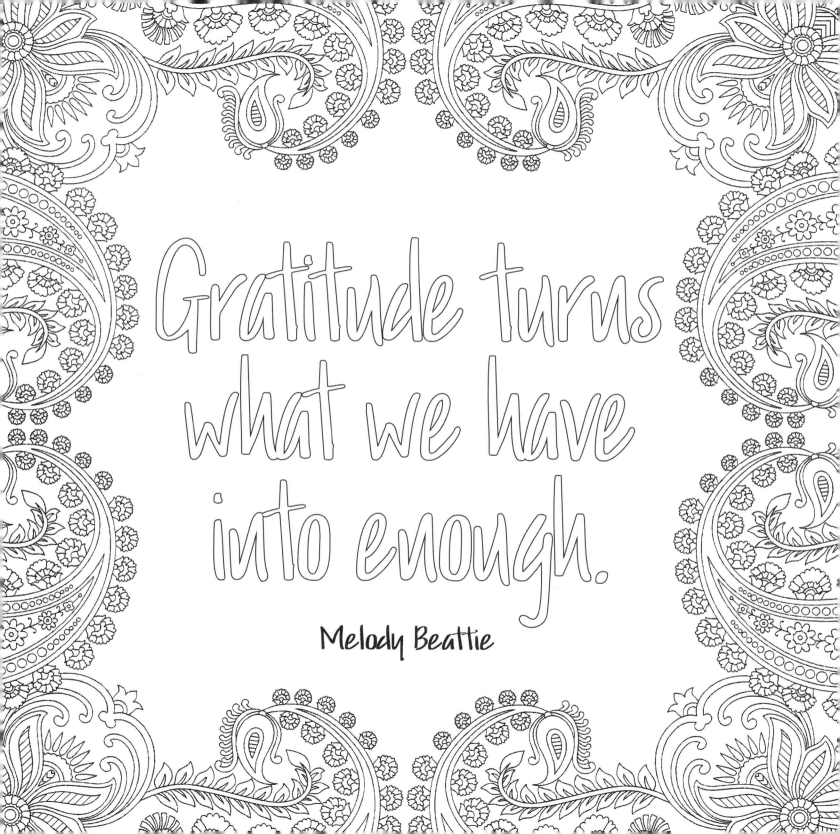

Gratitude turns
what we have
into enough.

Melody Beattie

Bloom where
you are
planted.

Hardships often prepare
ordinary people for an
extraordinary destiny.
C.S. Lewis

We shall never know all the good
that a simple smile can do.

Mother Teresa

Small deeds done
are better
than great deeds
planned.

Peter Marshall

Feeling gratitude
and not expressing it is
like wrapping a present
and not giving it.

William Arthur Ward

Never, never, never give up.

Winston Churchill

You are
the only you
in existence.
The world needs
your gifts.
your story.
your passion.
The world needs you!

A healthy attitude is contagious but don't wait to catch it from others. Be a carrier.

Tom Stoppard

Don't compare your weaknesses to someone else's strengths.

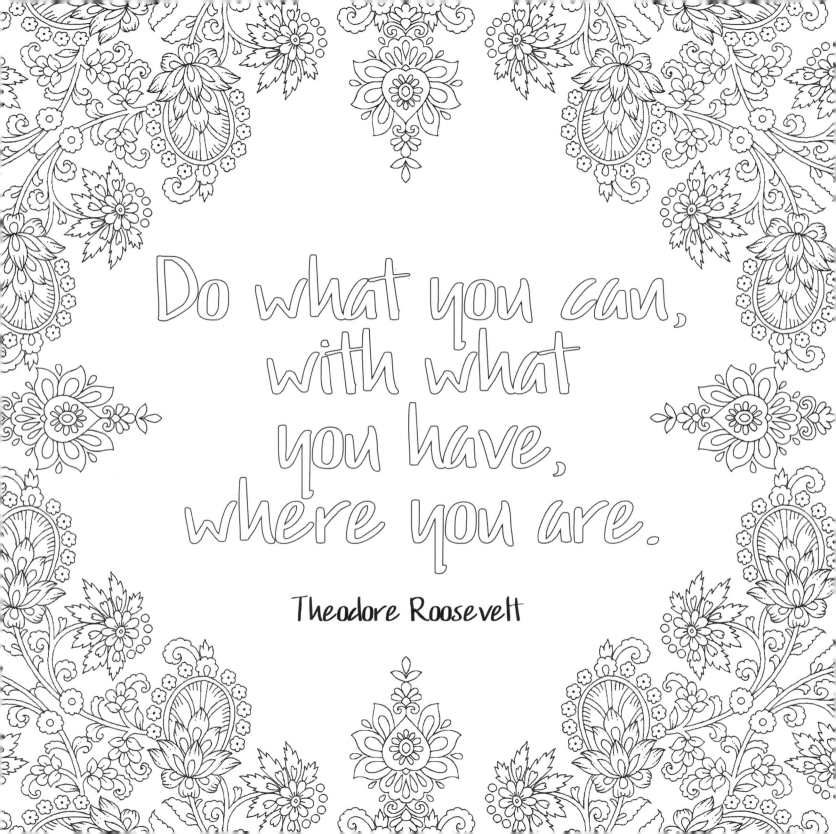

Do what you can,
with what
you have,
where you are.

Theodore Roosevelt

The secret of getting ahead is getting started.

Mark Twain

The smallest act of kindness
is worth more than
the grandest intention

Oscar
Wilde

How you make others feel about themselves says a lot about you.

We make a living by what we get
We make a life by what we give.

Winston S. Churchill

If you want to live an amazingly fulfilling life,
you must live for something bigger than yourself.

Don't
let
the things
you want
make you forget
the things
you
have.

No act
of kindness,
no matter
how small,
is ever wasted.

Aesop

In everything give thanks.

1 Thessalonians 5:18 NKJV

The best way to cheer yourself is to try to cheer someone else up.

Mark Twain

Life is 10% what happens to you
and 90% how you react to it.

Charles R.
Swindoll

Wherever you are, be all there.

Jim Elliot

Every day
may not be good,
but there is something
good in every day.

How wonderful it is
that nobody need wait
a single moment
before starting
to improve the world.
Anne Frank

There is always, always, always something to be thankful for.

No matter your circumstances,
no matter your situation,
if you start looking for
things to appreciate,
you'll begin to find them
all around you.

Comparison is the thief of joy.

Theodore Roosevelt

Being happy doesn't mean everything is perfect.

It means you've decided to see beyond the imperfections.

For it is in giving
that we receive.

Francis of Assisi

The happiest people are not those getting more, but those giving more.

H. Jackson Brown, Jr.